every single beast of my heart

every single beast of my heart

poems | pamela wax

Sheila-Na-Gig Editions

Cover art: iStock — Zoia Lunova
Cover design: Nan Bookless
Author photo: Ellen Joffe-Halpern

ISBN: 978-1-962405-63-8
Library of Congress Control Number: 2026934476

Sheila-Na-Gig Editions
Russell, KY
Hayley Mitchell Haugen, Editor
www.sheilanagigblog.com

Printed in the United States of America

Acknowledgments

Even a poetry collection takes a village. I have benefited from the wisdom of many gifted teachers who have helped me write, revise, and order the poems in this book: Travis Denton, Lisa Bellamy, Jennifer Martelli of blessed memory, Enzo Silon Surin, Jennifer Franklin, and Melissa Tuckey. I am grateful for the keen and insightful eyes of my poetry sisters: Kathie Jacobson, Janet Kaufman, Bernice Lewis, and Lily Jarman-Reisch, in addition to generous insights from treasured classmates in poetry workshops. Every comment has made me humbler and my work stronger.

I am grateful to the journals that originally published individual poems from this collection, sometimes in slightly different versions.

Artemis Journal: "The divo who stole the Tanglewood performance on a Sunday afternoon in July"
Barrow Street: "The First Two Questions Are One"
Book of Matches: "It wasn't a frog, but still, when I kissed"
Breakwater Review: "My husband prays I'll get Alzheimer's"
Broad River Review: "England Has a Ministry of Loneliness Now"
Broadkill Review: "Naming My Animals"
Burningword Literary Journal: "Chewing the Five Zen Remembrances"
Canary: "White Birches on the Hopper Trail"
CCAR Journal: "Gnawing Bones Dry"
Chautauqua: "Prokofiev's First Violin Sonata"
Connecticut River Review: "The Little Prince Said It First"
Crosswinds Poetry Journal: "My Grandfather Morris's Index Finger," "Pulling the Dead From the Pool"
Glimpse Poetry Magazine: "A Prayer for Disharmony," "Watching the Dead"
Gyroscope Review: "Ode to My Facial Hair"
The Healing Muse: "What Does it Say About Me"
Iron Horse Literary Review: "To my brother who left an 'I love you, when can we talk?' message one day, then jumped from a bridge the next"

Lily Poetry Review: "This Small, Wide World"
Lips Poetry Magazine: "A Small Lesson in Suffering"
Louisville Review: "Shea Stadium, 1972"
The MacGuffin: "The Great Big Indelible Tent of Us"
Mantis: "If You're Lucky"
The Massachusetts Review: "Mississippi Goddam," "See Jane run"
Mudfish: "Dear Sylvia"
Naugatuck River Review: "Dear Fertility"
New Verse News: "World Central Kitchen"
Nimrod: "*Monsterwörter* I Know, Though I May Never Visit Germany"
Nine Mile: "My Brother Skirts the Grim Reaper"
Oberon: "Starter Mothers"
One Art Poetry: "Birding With My Sister"
Pangyrus: "The Mighty Mississippi, August 29, 2021"
Passengers Journal: "At Pinto Lake"
Pensive Journal: "The Medium Channels Duende"
Pinch: "frog poem"
Poets' Billow: "1HLY 48"
Relief Journal: "The Angel Came to You as Picasso"
Rust & Moth: "*If you can't say anything nice,*" "These days I'm a scarecrow"
Schuylkill Poetry Journal: "Puffball"
Sheila-Na-Gig online: "Ode to My Husband's Aging Body"
Sixfold: "Talk Therapy"
Slippery Elm: "A seven-year study"
Solstice: "I watched my mother lurch"
Split Rock Review: "Still Radioactive in the Chernobyl Exclusion Zone"
Sunlight Press: "The Rabbi and I"
Valparaiso Poetry Review: "Training for My Next Life"
Worcester Review: "The Witch and the Rabbi"

The following poems appeared in *Starter Mothers* from Finishing Line Press: "Dear Fertility," "Starter Mothers," "The Little Prince Said It First," "The Angel Came to You as Picasso"

Let these five truths soak into your skin. You've always known them, because they've always been true. But best to remind yourself anyway.

—Koun Franz

Contents

I am of the nature to die

I will be separated and parted from all that is dear to me

My actions are the ground on which I stand;
I am my deeds

Of the Nature

I don't need more, my cousin confesses
over tea, one foot already out of this world.

She wants to go like her Babba
whose last words were, *Mamma,*

I want to come to you. She is nothing
if not pragmatic, spurns an afterlife,

has no plans to trick the Angel
of Doom. Between sips,

I invite her to close her eyes, recite
the Five Remembrances I use

to tame fears of extinction.
On hospice, she can't be Houdini.

You know what that's like,
she says on the phone

when her remaining brother dies.
Now, when a wisp of memory

summons her like a genie,
I grant her an afterlife

grounded in the deeds of her life,
pungent and honeyed as tea.

I am of the nature to age

Pulling the Dead From the Pool

—for Hulda

I'm reacquainted with death each morning,
as I skim corpses of mice, frogs, and moths
from my friend's pool. Before I swim, I discern
a sheeny copper beetle—Japanese—from a longhorn,
a leggy mosquito hawk from its namesake. Scooped
and soggy on the net, the bees make me saddest,
auguring the collapse of creation. I toss them
into the woods—a bit too casually, it seems now.
I watch an eagle circling against changeling clouds
as I backstroke, half-pondering his comeback from near-
extinction. My friend told me a moose jumped the fence
and drowned in her pool years ago. But I need no *memento*
mori, me, well into autumn, still swimming open-air,
racing against my fishy self, limber and cold-blooded.

To my brother who left an "I love you, when can we talk?" message one day, then jumped from a bridge the next

tell me, would you,
about the inscrutable darkness
and the glimmer
of us that couldn't lure you
to hold the living

about how you could go
headlong into the negative
space that must have welcomed
you in ways we did not

how you reconciled to that
moment on a Saturday, pre-dawn,
stood on a railing above a river
and said,
            now

how your *yes* outpaced
your *no* on the way down,
doubt spilling from your pockets
like loose change,
so much that you felt buoyant—
even for that instant

It wasn't a frog, but still, when I kissed

the red salamander, I thought I might get
lucky. He was from the same cold-blooded

family, the kind with the superpower to breathe
on land and submerged. I could use some luck,
and I believe in miracles, the anything-

can-happen sort. After he sidled up to my lips
in my friend's pool, I waited, half-expectant
and game. But when nothing happened, I noticed

he'd croaked, floating there. On the prowl
now for amphibians, I saw one give me
the once-over with his bulging 360-degree

eyes. I paddled over to find he was a lime-green
maple leaf curled over on himself with two
coppery Japanese beetles along for the cruise.

I dry-docked that ark poolside, and a sparrow—
white-crowned and bold—swooped down
just like that for a snack before taking off,

one still hanging from his mouth. I felt like Jonah
when he mourned the demise of gourds
that had kept him shaded from the sun.

The beetles hadn't saved me, but I'd salvaged
them. For nothing. I'm the same woman
who unceremoniously flushes spiders down

the toilet, though my aunt always said they make
a happy home. And now I'm inclined to rescue
them, along with dragonflies and birds and bees.

The Angel Came to You as Picasso

—for Ellen

Every child is an artist. The problem
is how to remain an artist once he grows up.
—Pablo Picasso

The philtrum just above your upper lip
where a finger fits so perfectly, any finger,
but, let's say, one on your left hand,

your painter's hand, the one that divulges
holy secrets on canvas—it was sculpted
by the angel Lailah when you were born,

that groove in your face, in mine,
in anyone's. In the womb she taught
you caverns within caverns of numinous

truths by the glow of a candle so you might
view all worlds in every dimension,
past and coming. She held a mirror

to your face, acquainting you
with splendor. You might have been born
haloed yourself, had she not tapped you

there with her own slender finger,
so you forgot everything but the desire
for all she'd stolen, a suspicion

that followed you like an echo.
So when you told me your dream,
the one where Picasso taught you

all he knew about art and laying brush
to palette—though you call it a visit,
even recalling the weight

and voice of him—and how fifty years
later, you're still recovering
all he revealed, I thought of Lailah

and how we spend our lives
tracking those kaleidoscope truths
she'd imparted *in utero*

telescoping back and forward, filaments
of light and color, as crumbs and whispers
on the scavenger hunt of our lives.

White Birches on the Hopper Trail

They are beautiful naked—
those buff, unadorned sentries
on the ready to welcome

snow with their bare
arms. *You stoic bastards,*
I think, impressed

by their macho, while I shiver,
bundled in down.
Some of them lie flat

and rotting, blankets of moss
under their birchy chins to stave
off chill, and I think

of nestling one there, down-
skin to bark-skin, layering
browned oak and maple

leaves to preserve my body
heat and to offer him
mine. Nothing salacious,

this simple love, as the winter
moths, out to feed off the decay, party
around us, fluttering like confetti.

Shea Stadium, 1972

the vendors hawked Rheingold and peanuts
when one hollered *Beeya heeya*
my father echoed *This is the place*
and swapped cups from the tray
for a wad of bills
Keep the change
then passed the beer
to the veterans of Post 146 in the seats around us
family friends with whom we'd shared a rented bus
from the Jersey suburbs
pooled bets on which inning
would score the most runs
and how Yogi might fare as the new manager

I asked about the black armbands on the left sleeves
of the uniforms
my father ran on about honoring the death of a comrade
the old manager who'd dropped dead

I was twelve   and gawky
hid puberty under layers of oversize
marveled at my father's largesse
dispensing dollars just like that
But Dad when he handed me a twenty to go buy 30
40-cent knishes   *Keep the change*
it's only money
and I didn't understand the *only* then
or that *this is*
the place   right here

now   and how dozing on the bus ride home
after the Mets beat the Pirates
I overheard pride
when he mentioned my good grades
how I'd amount to something

not have to stand on my feet
for twelve hours a day

my father who reclined on Sundays with WQXR
blasting all classical
a red and white can of Rheingold by his side
as he scanned the yard through binoculars
consulting his Peterson field guide only when an enigma
breezed in for a landing

my father who hid *The Joy of Sex*
right next to the encrypted Masonic handbook
in his nightstand where he thought
I'd never find them

my father who didn't want to know
I was blooming under my layers
almost ready to decipher adult mysteries
like loyalty to comrades
or generosity to those who aren't blood

The Witch and the Rabbi

Four decades after we drank in Shakespeare
and the Tate on a semester abroad,
she steeps dandelion in a chipped mug

at her kitchen table. *It's good for you—not
a weed.* She dresses like a creature
of the forest to welcome Imbolg, when winter

is pregnant with summer, and in flowing red
robes on full moons. She midwifes all station
stops on the lifecycle—lullabies for birthing

mothers, ululations for the dying, and points
to her shelves of jars for ailments in any
of our eleven organ systems—would-be potions

of nettles, yarrow, feverfew. I buy all her tick
bite remedies. I think about Salem and crucibles,
how a crone alone in the woods like my friend

would end in flames or at the end of a rope. I think
of *Macbeth,* those wayward sisters who prophesied
trouble, the biblical *There shalt not be a witch*

amongst you, how my friend carries that history
of suspicion. I think about my Jewish rituals
under open sky, hands stretched toward sliver moons

to call down blessing for the new month, palm fronds,
myrtle, and willow paraded in sacred dance
each fall, incanting ancient Hebrew, eating al fresco

in fragile huts decked with branch and fruit—
but only for a week each year, the paucity of it,
I think now. I, too, show up at deathbeds and rites

for babies, coming-of-age, and legal handfasts.
But she stands closer to the pulse of the whole
broken world of it, its rhythms and disruptions,

the rose-breasted grosbeak perched on her feeder,
the bees and swallowtails she nurtures from near
extinction. She hands me a shovel to dig out Siberian

irises for my own garden, a gesture to honor
both wisdom and the Bard. Iris appears in five
of his plays, cryptic, double-edged. She bears tidings

both good and nasty from the gods, creates
both the tempest and the rainbow that follows—
arcane like we Jews, artful like us witches.

Starter Mothers

—for Susan

About 87 miles southeast of Brussels, the residents of a living library are fermenting away.

—Smithsonianmag.com

They come to Sankt Vith from Peru
and Malta, Japan, and the States
for safekeeping, speaking a language
that bubbles up as a beige glob
of bacteria when flour meets water.
Unlike me, they are mothers, all
125 of them, catalogued and shelved,
refrigerated and honored. They are fed
every two months from a reserve
of flour bequeathed by their bakers
for perpetual care. A mother
from Greece is kept alive by holy water
infused with basil. A Swiss mother
has discovered a long-lost cousin
from Mexico—they share the same wild
Torulaspora present in none
of the others. Blame it on the altitude,
or on a universal Venn diagram
that connects everything. I recognize
the lust for immortality.

Some claim to be centuries old,
but who's to say for sure.
Their aim is self-perpetuation,
these starters, and their history
is baked into exodus tales
the world over, carried as family
heirlooms across passes and oceans.
Fortune seekers carried flour
and mother from the Arctic

north, became fabled gold miners
cuddling San Francisco sourdoughs
to keep them warm on cold nights.
I, myself, have felt the burden
of such a mother. *It's hard*
to kill her, my friend said
when I forgot to feed the one
she'd gifted me.

I know mother lust
and death lust, too,
like unfermented dust,
sterile dreams of wheat rot
in my mouth, sour and raw.

Dear Fertility

What have you done with my eggs,
the ones that dropped inchoate
and bloody into the toilet
for forty-nine years?
Had you fooled my birth control du jour,
been prankster enough
to pull one over God and me,
I might have been eye candy
at Stop & Shop's check-out, crowning
the cover of *The Enquirer,* a miracle
mother at sixty.

Instead, I was only Dr. D.'s private
wonder. I'd be lying if I didn't tell you
I almost wish there'd been a deus ex
machina flying from the wings
to explain your longevity—how
I'd missed my true calling, or maybe

that my child would have been a *lamed-vavnik,*
one of the thirty-six in a generation
who hold up the world like Malala
and Greta, Emma, and Darnella,
and it's all my fault there's no messiah.

Perhaps I botched the plot line
through my intransigence, my only
pregnancy aborted by choice,
so you've shadowed me ever since,
a loyal temptress, hanging on
for a different ending. Maybe

you decided to keep me company
from the beginning, the first page
of our memoir when I was eleven,

away at camp, and my father waxed
poetic about my womanness.

Or maybe you liked how my mother
never officially bid you adieu, how
she died at sixty-four, and when I cleaned
out her drawers, I found her diaphragm
intact, though her periods stopped
with the chemo in her forties.

You assumed I'd join the ranks
of my friends who'd chosen
single motherhood with sperm donors
in their thirties. In my forties,
you disapproved when I told
my new husband I'd never
have children with him
because of the schizophrenia
in his tree. I stand by that.
I suspect you had valid reasons,
though my nutritionist simply blamed
your tenacity on cows, made me go cold
turkey on dairy. It didn't help.
But I miss you now. And Dr. D's attention,
how she marveled each time she drew blood.

Ode to My Husband's Aging Body

How it stoops under weight of skull,
wobbling and nodding, a chicken
pecking for seeds, bobbing for apples.
He is not a chicken. No, he is curved

like a gooseneck lamp, but less bendy,
fossilizing into downward dog. He bears
the burden of sky, an Atlas defeated,
shuffling off-balance like a *shicker,*

stubbly, his vanity gone the way
of the woolly mammoth. He is softer
now, folds of skin I knead like dough.
I play harp to his broody Saul.

Songful, viscid as a peach, he's raw
as a quahog pulsing on the half-
shell. I'm drawn to his quick.
We are a law of gravity—like the heft

of hand on thigh, of tongue to salty
cheek, strains of portent. We read
walls, he and I, numbered
and lettered. Return him to me

there, if he'll have me, Cronos,
you wrecking ball of time.
O, Hades, o, Pluto, o, Kali, o, Mot,
our nightmares impersonate fits of sleep.

Reconnaissance

My husband calls his missions
forensics. I call them *surveillance.*
If I'm late, he'll case the clothesline—
no bathing suit, I'm swimming;
bathing suit, he dragnets the streets.
If he's angling for a late-life career
with the Feds, I remind him I'm the one
hooked on thrillers, crushing
on undercover assassins whose coattails
I ride into fifth columns and terror cells,
smoking out old Nazis or Russian
moles, ever spying over my shoulder
for liars-in-wait. We're of an age
to worry if the other lies in some ditch
belly-up, gasping for air, easy
marks for thugs or heatstroke.
At night I keep a mirror beside me
under the covers, lift it to his nostrils
if I can't hear him breathe.
I practice for when the CIA comes
knocking for a mild-mannered female
rabbi to front some big sting.

Puffball

It gleamed like a volleyball in our backyard. Smooth, white, round. My husband mentioned it to the neighbor across the street. *Our kids play softball,* she said. We waited for someone else to claim it, but it was still there the next day when I watered my zucchini, and the day after that when I took the kitchen scraps to the compost heap. It was there as my husband crossed the lawn to his workshop in the barn, and when I took the blue camping chair out of the garage to savor the autumn panorama we're lucky enough to boast from our yard. We didn't realize it was a living thing until it was already brown, its spores spewing forth like a dust storm when my husband mowed into it. All of a sudden that aging fungus became a metaphor for hindsight of every kind, and I was glad for that afternoon I spent watching the light play over the Berkshire hills, and I grieved all over again for the dead I'd lost before knowing I should say goodbye, and I looked at my husband, all of his gray, which made me look in the mirror at mine. *Poof,* I said, *I'm of the nature to age,* remembering my first gray hair over three decades before, how I'd pulled it out and taped it to the bathroom mirror, a philosophy to brush my teeth to, while hoping against hope for foresight.

Ode to My Facial Hair

You were not the inheritance of my dreams.
My mother (Harriette, daughter of Harry)
paid a pretty penny for your death
by electrolysis at the hands of the widow
Mildred—our appointments scheduled
back-to-back, a mother-daughter special.
I took matters into my own hands, impatient
for quick fixes. Plucking. Shaving. Waxing.
Epilating. Burning my chin raw
with noxious creams named Sally Hansen
and Neet to kill you, my intractable roots,
invasive, hardy, perhaps immortal—
determined to see me as the bearded lady
at the circus. Face it. You've won the war,
showing up every morning uninvited,
sending me at midnight to 24-hour
Walgreens' in distant cities when I forget
to pack my tweezers. But when I'm old
and dozing in the hallway of some
nursing home, like my hirsute Grandma
Sadie, tell me, who will tend to you,
my pretties, my offspring—gray
and wiry, virile and resilient—tendrilling
your way to eternity?

I am of the nature to grow ill

These days I'm a scarecrow

posted like the clothesline frayed and weathered

exposed to elements with no mercy

one arm pointing skyward the other heartward.

I hang here guarding a dust bowl of dead things barren

birdless my lips stitched into a black line

three dots three dashes three dots

no one left to read them.

Talk Therapy

"Oysshprekhn—"
my husband said
once, when I recited
my poems aloud
again and again
for breath
            and sound
                        and meter,
to trim the fat
and carve them
lean—

"after the camps—
the ones who talked
to themselves."

He was not impugning
my mental health,
nor theirs. It's how
they healed
themselves, he said.

"You remind me of them."

Prokofiev's First Violin Sonata

—for Julie

My friend anchors the violin
with her chin, her head turned
slightly left, bow in her right
hand. She nods to the pianist
to begin. She calls upon her own
despair to interpret the composer's
intention. The notes of the score—
steeped in the gore of gulags
and wet kisses from Judas—
foreshadow tyrannies
that still subsist on iron hands
and cold sweat. My friend plays
the slithering scales like wind
in a graveyard. She hears
the bones rattle in the hall.

Spin Cycle

My brother's madness spun faster than mine, something with vortex. He said I was normal, like the setting on his Maytag. *No agitation,* he winked, *no pearl.* I kept tabs on his cycle, while mine—trifling, like small talk—rumbled offshore in the Atlantic. Set to *Dervish,* his hurricaned toward landfall, blew our whole house to sea, front door slamming still.

The Leaves Fell Early That Year

—in memory of Cindy

With that opening gambit, I knew
Hemingway foreshadowed someone's
untimely farewell—the troops emptying
out with the dust, the premature fall.
I could also predict that the star-crossed
lovers in Verona and the carefree prince
of the apple towns on Fern Hill
were all doomed from the get-go.

I didn't need to major in English, art history,
or film to hear the threat on the horizon
in the score from *Jaws* or notice how Brueghel
painted a farmer in the foreground to prove
how easily the tragedy of a fall can be ignored,
especially one brimming in hubris.

When my friend jumped, her son strapped
snuggly against her breasts for all eight stories,
he survived. He's ten now, afraid
of roller coasters and bumper cars,
dreaming himself a superhero who parachutes
into war-torn regions to rescue baby
kangaroos or mothers with rockets' red glare
firing in their postpartum brains.

I think of her now that I have a brother
who jumped and died,
and a niece and a nephew who survived,
home asleep at the time.

But I have a question about foreshadowing—
whether I could have, should have, followed
the crumbs she and my brother left

scattered on my hallway table, waiting
for an English major in search
of a thesis topic, sitting right there
next to my family photos and the daily *Times*.

My husband prays I'll get Alzheimer's

so when

I forget him I'll

fall for the stranger

he's become.

The Poet at Her Desk

Of course, it's never tidy,
or rather: once organized,
re-clutters. Dog-eared
scraps, pens loud
in colors. For work.
For serious play. In which
I doodle. Or procrastinate.
With which I place one word
beside another. Recite them
aloud. Exchange one
for its assonance. Then scratch
it out. Which makes me an artist.
Or a dilettante. How I dabble.
Like my marriage. Splash
about. Float just above the churn.
In an ark. The desk, the ark
are just metaphors. I feed
my animals one word at a time.
Love. Forgive. Someday. Maybe.

Hand Drum

He lured me, hands
precise and dexterous—carnal
combination of finger, wrist
and arm—that held drum
against body, pranced the tight
animal skin of it, coaxing
shudder and moan, fingertips
open for higher pitches, the snarl
of bass with palm. *Good*
with his hands, my friends joked
knowingly when he made
our kitchen table, our bed
with shelves for overflow books,
shutters for our windows.
When I blinked, he couldn't
remember the day of the week
or how to turn the oven off. His
tremoring hands rouse me
not, but suffice for dishes—
stubborn particles forgiven. I dust
off the drum, how the rhythm syncs
his brain, sends tremors down my spine.

I watched my mother lurch

back and forth
in an open car door

when Mrs. L. dropped her home
after playing bridge. How

she swung from its frame
as the car reversed. How she toppled

with a head bleed, epileptic
fits for the rest of her life. I majored

in her rhythmic quirks, her rubbing
the fingers of her right hand,

the lolling of her tongue. The foot
itching to dance at some ghostly

nightclub, and the tapping of a teaspoon
against the steaming mug, coffee

lukewarm by the time she came home,
glazed and guileless.

How I'd hurry my friends
from the room even if she hadn't lost

her bowels. Even if she weren't
                    on the floor in melted ice, freezer

door open. The shame.
                    Even now, it chafes with the clink

of a glass at a wedding,
                    or my husband's restless

leg, or a cat pawing,
                    kneading, persistent, cadent.

A Small Lesson in Suffering

Perhaps you had a once-upon
like mine, your mother on the edge
of your bed, spinning Grimm
into something shiny, a thermometer
clenched in your backside.

I liked how Red Riding Hood
wouldn't let fear of the forest hold
her back from destiny, how Goldilocks
found the nuance at the center of extremes.

I wanted the gumption
to enter my neighbors' house
unbidden, open the refrigerator, test
the spring in their beds, walk
to Grandmother's without a chaperone.

Even at five, I felt uneasy lying
like that on my belly. I counted
under my breath as high as I could,
asked my mother how long
until I got old and died. *A long,*
long time, she said, though I could count
to a hundred in seconds.

Of course, this may be a lie—the parallel
I drew between violation and mortality,
between myself and a girl
devoured by a wolf passing as kin.

I relished the hand stroking my back,
the soothing voice of that woman
who mothered me to health, that childhood
that was neither idyll nor horror,
just somewhere between tall tales
and short stories, between cold
shoulders and mounting tempers.

Take It In

Preamble: A traveller, wandering from place to place, saw a
palace in flames. *How could it be that the palace has no owner?*
—*Midrash Genesis Rabbah* 39:1

To write about a world on fire,
i start before i knew it was.

Lake Hopatcong: the rocking of a boat.
my body holds the memory.
a bat brushes my forehead, catches my hair while i sleep.
cast of a rod. the arc of the line from wrist
to red-and-white bobber. the plop, rippling.
wait for a tug. practice listening. practice sight.
shadows trip over light at daybreak.
blessed the One who distinguishes day from night
when i can tell white from sky-blue, a grebe from a duck.

T.I.: Family shorthand for *Take it in*. Originally used to discourage pointing. As in *T.I.*, with a nod toward the woman in the bikini sunning herself with a reflector across the street. We thought this meant, *Shouldn't she be wearing a one-piece?* Maybe it meant, *Does she know the sun can kill?* Current usage: Be curious. Stay open.

wait for the tug. i become the grebe while i wait.
the sun rises.
i become the mist on the surface,
the northern pike undulating beneath the ripple
the sounds of solitude, subtle as tiptoes—
lapping. flapping. rustles. slithers. gulps.

the fish, hooked, suffocates,
its squeal, mute.
its eye glares up at me.
~~guilty as charged~~.

T.I. (point finger at everyone.)

my body holds this memory—
    a slide, the whoosh into Lake Waywayanda,
        my father at the bottom to catch, then toss me
        deeper,
            squealing,
        where i breathe underwater, amphibious,
            to emerge without sputtering.
        Way Way Yonder, he points.
            the view of the mountain. *See it? T.I.*

Still Radioactive in the Chernobyl Exclusion Zone

—for Aryeh

Less than a hundred people in a thousand
square miles, but the wildlife
is back: brown bears, bison, lynx, elk,

even white-tailed eagles, extinct
before the meltdown. They burrow
and fly, hunt and mate, adapting

to explosions in their DNA. *It's not like*
a miracle, my friend says. *It is one.*
Like the sunflowers grown to extract

toxins from the soil there, like sunflowers
planted to celebrate Ukraine's nuclear
disarmament ten years later, like those

planted now, solidarity blooming
across the globe, like the blaze of sun
up my arm when that same friend—to whom

I'd said good-bye for four years each time
I saw him post-apocalypse—called from Sloan-Kettering
to say the cancer we thought fatal is cured.

I am of the nature to die

Naming My Animals

Those little red ones you like,
my husband said, pressing
his forefinger to the joint
in the middle of his thumb
to form a small circle.

He wants me to know what's
on sale for my rebound trip
to Stop & Shop. *Cherries?*
I ask. He nods, *I'm not good*
at fruits and vegetables.

It's true. His merchandise is tools.
He woodworks his way through
sanders and planes, can see
saws and squares, adzes
and lathes where I observe

mere machine and blade. I name
things of nature, labelling
clouds nimbus or cumulus,
contrasting heart-shaped leaves—
linden vs. aspen, mild-mannered

ladybugs with badass Asian Lady
Beetles. I know my apples—Gala,
Empire, Mac—and Dinosaur
from Red Russian kale,
both prehistoric. I try to classify

each tiered layer of grief—
its raging undercurrents of horror
and remorse, despair that douses
each morning's blaze, reptilian
flights and freezes that hiss

anonymous curses at the waning
moon. Nuances abound,
and yet I am still trying to name
all my animals—every single
variegated beast of my heart.

Training for My Next Life

—in memory of Chip

To shoot false morels, deathcaps, destroying
angels, even the fly agaric—that fairy-tale
toadstool, red with little white dots—
all deadly, beguiling as hell from above
and head-on, I squat close to forest floor.
I know bracket fungi, turkey tails cascading
from tree trunks, and witches' butter, bound
to downed hardwood, photogenic now
after late summer rain. Yesterday at shiva,
my husband mimed Chip, arms skyward,
lying flat on a downtown sidewalk, aiming
his Nikon at a bird seen best from that angle.
So today I sprawled, a mud angel, to commune
from below, the vantage of spores.

The Mighty Mississippi, August 29, 2021

What alarmed you, O sea, that you fled?
River Jordan, that you ran backward?

—Psalms 114:5

After the thrill-flash in the storm-dark,
chant-count your prayers, a child's wish
for crash-boom: *One Mississippi, two*
Mississippi, three… rhythmic until the measured
truth cracks, redounding in glass panes,
floorboards, and our bones   the epiphany of an eye,
a storm, a blink of a mile or five, or one too distant
for danger.   Nature runs its course:
            The Gulf Stream is warm and swift,
            birds migrate, you age, loved ones die,
            matter cannot be created or destroyed,
            the Ol' Man flows south to the delta
until it doesn't. Until Ida runs
its course into the ground,   and your dead
splash all around you, laughing.

Watching the Dead

I sit with my friend
in the hours before her funeral.
Her soul, newly bewildered,
must not be alone. There's a buzz
from the lights, a stream
of traffic flowing along
West Main outside the mortuary.
            And the hum—
my own need to find what glitters
in this witnessing. I imagine her
corpse-posed body inside the plain
pine box, rub the lid of it up
and down the vaulted length
of her, and coo, as if stroking her
back, knowing full well she faces
heavenward. I linger at the raised
star, a reminder to *Honor*
father, mother. I trace the *lameds,*
the *vavs,* the *alephs,* and *tavs* needled
into the seasoned robe draping
the coffin like royalty. I flip
through the psalter for length
of days and vagaries. I find valleys
of shadows and withering grass.

The worst-case scenario is confirmed at the River Forest police station the day after Mother's Day

and you thank God your parents are not alive. 23 escorts
you, yea, as you walk through the shadows
until his body is recovered. *There's something wrong*

when people disappear, Girlyman blares. *Damn straight,*
you wail, popping one sleeping pill, then another,
to ensure repose in degraded pastures, and dream

of black raspberry ice cream at Applegate Farm,
where your brother chooses chocolate, dripping
onto his shirt. *It's only a thing,* your mother scolds

when your father yells, and in the back seat your brother
plucks the x's from the outside of your Cat's Cradle
to make Soldier's Bed, and your mother winks at you.

23 is the only psalm she knew by heart.

My Brother Skirts the Grim Reaper, 2010

He crosses the street with a four-year-old
princess and Thomas the Tank Engine,
also four. His proud father outfit suits
him, his broad smile the superhero
of the photo. His children skip
in the crosswalk, dangling their treats,
unaware of the dirty bag of tricks
eight years down the road. Only now
I spot the tall figure trailing him—
black cloak, metallic ghoul mask, sword
in his right hand. Eerily close
for Midwest decorum. I know those tales
of the Angel of Death—how
he can be duped or bargained with. How,
through good turns or devoted study,
he can be delayed. Once a sage stole
the sword to end time as we know it—
but God intervened, the world not yet ripe
for paradise. I think now of my brother's close
shave that Halloween, no sense of a tragic ending
to come, delivered—was it the joy?—
while that Destroyer bided time,
breathing down his neck.

My Grandfather Morris's Index Finger

Created to point the way
westward towards Europe
and a new world beyond that,
made, perhaps, to fiddle
or pluck the likes of Tchaikovsky,
to trace the folds of his wife's
privates, to teach his sons square
knots and bowlines, to string cat's
cradles with ten grandchildren,
to wag in the face of injustice
and a god who does not exist, aiming
instead for Polaris, *There! Shining*
there! and the Communist compass
of his working-man's phalanx,
made to be worked to the bone.

All flesh and knuckle in extremity—
the forefinger of a right hand,
appended once to a *boychik,*
bar mitzvah age (were religion not
the opium of his people). So *meshuga*
in his head, this Morris, from fear
of cantonist conscription, he chopped
it free from its four closest compatriots
to escape his sentence of hup-hup
servitude to imperial appetite. Self-
mutilated to claim manhood,
he mustered the other Jew-boys to stick
fingers in the eyes of the regime.
It hurt less than you might think, less
than pulling a trigger for the Tsar.
Now only phantom pain, hearty scraps
for the chickens, who clucked,
but could not refuse its clots and veins.

Gnawing Bones Dry

—for Sandy

The chicken bones on her plate
were picked clean—flesh, skin,
even gristle, a disappearing act
so thorough I wondered
about my friend's less public
compulsions. The neat pile
of remains stoked a memory
from another guest—*A neighbor*
hid my mother during the war.

Over dessert, he told us how
his mother, skin and bones,
thumbed her nose
at the neighbor's pork,
still thinking God might save her.
How the neighbor smuggled
herself into the ghetto,
where a starving rabbi tendered
a Solomonic compromise
to preserve both life and law—
Tell her to eat the meat,
but not enjoy so much
she sucks down to the bone.

That tidy mass on my friend's
dinner plate was no mere
carcass from a chicken now.
I imagined them cremains
or like ribs, skulls, femurs
in some mass grave, or maybe
whole skeletons laying
dignified like my parents
in their plain pine coffins.

Those bones—a history lesson
in lamentation imbibed with mother's
milk—were an ironic whiff
of a *next-year-in-Jerusalem,*
somewhere-over-the-rainbow
kind of hope. That hill of bones
was a Janus of dualities, double-
edged like Israelite flat bread
made in a hurry—symbol
of both slave and non-
at the same time, like Ezekiel's
bones in the valley, clanking to life.

Mississippi Goddam

Have mercy on this land of mine.
—Nina Simone

Dobbs vs. the iconic pink house
stucco
its green metal roof
on N. State Street
in Jackson MS
Ms.
Miss(ed)

period (her/everywoman's story)
misruled mischief
goddam misery somebody say a prayer

everybody we're stuck
between a rock and a birthstool
crowning long before the midwife
can arrive with silphium
to end it
or birthwort to help
her
along

See Jane run

The Jane Collective was a cohort of Chicago activists who helped pregnant women obtain abortions and, eventually, performed the abortions themselves.

—Smithsonian Magazine

far from Dick naughty naughty Dick
see Father raise big voice see Mother cry

see big city see Jane hide
see Jane hold baby Sally cupboards bare

see Jane see red seek more Janes
help Janka
Juanita
Gianna
Jan

see big men wear blue
red lights go round and round
hear Janes
raise big voices shout *no*

witness *no* run
down Janes' cheeks between their legs
inside their song
a run-on sentence all life long

The divo who stole the Tanglewood performance on a Sunday afternoon in July

was a male finch, red-headed,
    serenading his sweetheart
        from the rafters of the Shed.

His birdsong sprinkled
    Blessed are those who mourn
        with whimsy and brio—

Poignant, wrote *The Globe* reviewer—
    the bird's warbling voice laying its own
        counterpoint from above
            to the Brahms below.

The finch hadn't read the program notes,
    couldn't know the requiem had been composed
        to honor the maestro's mother's death.

The chorus, one hundred vocalists strong—
    its luminous swell of sound—grounded
        the soprano, the baritone, the intruders' chirrups.

I named these lovebirds Harriette and Herb
    after my parents who raised us on the Three B's
        and Sinatra, and who sat hand in hand
            in concerts like this one.

My sister, beside me, didn't see
    we were brought there by some design,
        our father unashamed to bellow his lust
            before a throng of melophiles.

Still, she joined me in *bravos* and ovation
    for that couple who scorned knells and threnodies
        to croon *die Liebe* unrehearsed.

Dear Sylvia,

It was JFK's demise at 46 not yours

that hung heavy in the curtains

with my mother's Kents when I was three

Cronkite's voice caught at 2:38 eastern standard

cut into *As the World Turns* on CBS and everything

is still lopsided even after my father came home

to hug us mid-day It never recalibrated

for your one-year-old who kicked off at 47

by hanging You were 30 when you reclined

into that oven I learned about you from Phyllis

my professor death by carbon monoxide at 36

like your friend Anne in the garage

Phyllis's daughter died at 23

gored by her boyfriend in a church parking lot

My friend Cindy plunged from a window

her 10-month old strapped to her chest

He survived but who knows

And consider my niece   my nephew

five years after my brother   53

sailed from the Skyway   over the Calumet

It was dark   nearly dawn

What does it say about me

that, when asked about rock
as a metaphor for God—
Rock of Ages, Rock of Israel,
my Rock and my Redeemer, my Rock
in Whom there is no wrong—

I try to think of God
as one of the smooth, pastel
beach stones I haul in my car to leave
on the graves of my loyal
dead, or as the Vishnu Schist
of the Grand Canyon, catching
light and color when sun rises
or turns in for the night,
or as the red rock of Zion, oxidized
and bloody, because bloodshed
is relentless—
but I can't.

I'm partial to dead trees,
not the ones leafless
in winter, sure to revive
in spring, but those hollowed out,
skeletal and grayed.
I've taken hundreds of photos
of their spindly arms reaching
toward me like an arborescent
angel of death. Chancing
on one so mortal in the woods
can bring me to prayer,
gulping for breath.

God for me is the fleeting,
not the forever. *I am of the nature
to die,* one of the five Zen gospels I pocket
for plain truth and honest reporting
as my body sags with its expenditures
and investments, trying to purchase
wisdom hard as oak and bone.

I will be separated and parted
from all that is dear to me

Umbrella

Not a miniature one you'll find

in a Rum Runner at a Tiki bar,

bright colored paper and toothpick.

Nor *wagasa,* a full-sized parasol

of *washi* paper held aloft by a geisha

in a Japanese block print

or as *kabuki* prop, closed

to impersonate a cane,

opened to play a house

or a ceremonial accessory—

red for weddings, white for death.

It's not the Poor Man's Umbrella

I ducked beneath in Costa Rica,

heart-shaped leaves up to six

feet across. Nor is it the collapsible

kind, small enough to fit a purse

or briefcase, on the ready for downpour.

I'm talking about the tan one—

overlapping black-and-white circles

in assorted sizes, its butter-smooth

handle sized to my grip—bought four

decades ago in Kyoto and left

behind five years later in Cambridge,

the one I still think about

when I think about the phenomenon

of lost umbrellas. If you're like

the average person, you'll lose

several in your lifetime. Today

I saw an ad: *Left your umbrella behind?*

Your phone will alert you.

It uses Bluetooth.
I've never grown so attached

again that I'd need such an alert.

But I'd needed it then,

before I was practiced in losing,

before exposure to elements

extreme—and brutal chance.

England has a Ministry of Loneliness Now

Have you seen the old girl who walks the streets of London,
dirt in her hair and her clothes in rags?
—Ralph McTell, "Streets of London"

When I'm chilled by true sorrow
bowed in D minor, I hear the woman
next door, fall of '81, how she haunted
our London boarding house,
the middle of night.
How she did not play, but keened
her violin, a banshee wiled
from the Otherworld. I imagined
how she cradled her instrument,
nuzzling it with her chin—a child
she'd lost, a lover never known,
the world she might nudge into taking
notice. I'd pass her, wordless, on the way
to the shared bath, her gray hair greasy,
a mouse scurrying back to her own four walls.

How I lay rigid, icy on the other side
of the double doors between her parlor room
and mine, privy to her rites of exorcism
or flagellation. Was she Rachel, refusing
to be comforted for her children? One
of the Heliades, lamenting her brother
on the banks of the Eridanus for eternity?
La Llorona, abandoned, vengeful—or worse,
Ophelia, mad, on the brink of self-murder?

On that semester abroad, I, twenty, watched
tragedy play out on the stages of the Old Vic
and the National, clueless to the scheming
of lived despair, its savagery, as she drew
her bow each night across a body,
wooden and hollow.

Endangered Species

—June 24, 2024

A memorial candle for *Roe* burns
like reflux on my kitchen table.
I post a yellow-faced emoji
shedding its single blue tear
on my Facebook page, title it

Dobbs, 2 years. A stranger
posts a 19th-century map of states
in response, a graph of bison
slaughter. In support or protest,
I can't be sure. I blow the image

up. A mere 6 orange dots
represent all of 1000 survivors
where millions once shook
the ground. The buffalo population
dwindled, herd by herd. I study

that map, wonder where the loci
of our survival might present 50, 100,
200 years from now. I try not to think
of Atwood's Gilead, or the Bible's
6 cities of refuge. But how can I

not—me, who once marched like doom
in handmaid's red cape and hood
through halls of justice? The buffalo
blood bellows like my sisters, beasts
of burden, holy things calling our names.

At Pinto Lake,

—for Aryeh

I heard but did not see

the bittern, his distinctive gulp
almost like a bullfrog's. Pineapple

undertones wafted as I crushed
wild chamomile underfoot

with live oaks above me,
their arms extended as wide

as they are tall, covered in dangling
Spanish moss like bluish phantom

hair. My guide pointed to a tarp-
covered *ofrenda* across the lake,

built by a woman who saw Jesus
there on the bark of a tree.

The Parks Department allows
it to stand. Inside: lit candles,

a bowl of water, paper banners
that float on the breeze

like the spirits they are meant
to greet. The candles will guide

the dead to this place, the water
will slake them. The pilgrimage

is long, harrowing. My friend,
alive just a few miles away,

will soon journey among them.
I brought him a book of Japanese

death poems and one of Hasidic
teachings on hope and joy.

He meditates his way to acceptance,
one Zen truth at a time: *I will be*

separated from everything…
I send him a wind chime to guide

his way—may it arrive
before sound, his last sense, leaves.

A Prayer for Disharmony

O Orchestra, storm! Enough
with the crowd-pleasers playing
it safe. Smoke your rhythmic roll
of reed and brass, conduct
concertos charged electric. Pour
bubbly from fluted glasses, piccolo
us, horn us, pluck us saxy. Swing signs
and cymbals, vibrato
our steel-stringed bones.
Blow us from our cushioned
seats, and movement me vivace
from despair to action, timpani
without tip-toe. No more
lento-gravé, composing
me to death, a broken motif
on repeat, all pomp, no
circumstance. I crave
dissonance, tempest
and prestissimo, roused
to discordant halls of protest,
on my feet, applauding a new world,
symphonic. 1812 Overture me,
cannons without Pachelbel,
violins to beat the tacet rest
from my tautly-strung chambers,
a piece of hymn from my B-flat heart.

If you can't say anything nice

is how my mother would begin—
so I, like an unassuming mollusk,
maybe an octopus, would compress
myself into a spiraled conch
perched on my inner continental
shelf, where the not-nice lingers,
            submerged,
descending as silt and sediment
            to the seabed—
an abyssal plain,
a volcanic hill,
            hideous,
layers of calcareous ooze
            percolating,
a hydrothermal vent of all
I was not allowed to air
on the sandy surface where I seethed.

Adjacent Graves, Mount Solomon Cemetery

If bones could pray
they'd surely squeeze their socket eyes
in their skully breathless tombs.

And if bones had humor
for sure they'd tickle
one another with their dry
funny bony wit.

And if bones could weave
they'd knit their fingers
fourth to fourth
until wed   alive
and holy whole.

As I knew them

before   alone   alone.

frog poem

enough lamentation. i'm done
brooding on my brother's last
phone message and gruesome

end, done romanticizing us
thick and clichéd as thieves,
when we were both too young

to know anyone who'd steal
their own life. i'm moving on
to new material—a frog poem

without mention of suicide
or sleeping pills that guard
my derailments in the dark.

this poem boasts panoramic vision
and features no self-recrimination.
i'm taking on a well-camouflaged

creature who packs ultrasonic cries
inaudible to human ears and neither
resembles nor incriminates

brother or self. rather, i portray
a glistening cold-water vertebrate
who can enter a state of torpor

and remain inactive for months
during extreme conditions. what
i'm writing is tail-less,

an only child with no siblings,
no need for trigger warnings,
nor any attempts to mimic

a low-pitch vibrato
croaking *i love you* into a phone,
before asking forgiveness

for prehistoric wrongs. my poem
concerns a frog facing extinction.
i'm thrilled to report how

my utterly new material exploits
an unprecedented ecological niche:
it is amphibious, able to breathe

in heaven, underwater, as well
as on earth. it concerns a handsome
would-be prince of a frog, long-legged,

accomplished at jumping, who enters
limbo from the Skyway Bridge, and sticks
the landing with his webbed hind feet.

Monsterwörter I Know, Though I May Never Visit Germany

In the *Zeitgeist*
                the ghost forgets to stay dead,
settles down,
becomes the spirit of the times.

After *Kindergarten*
                you learn to get by without nap time
until middle age.

Your *Doppelgänger*
                is named Amy.
People call you by her name.
You look for her all your life.

Untermenschen are packaged
                in the language of infestation,
all manner of vermin—rats
and roaches creeping after your women,
your *Kinder.*

They call it *Vergangenheitsaufarbeitung*
                or *Vergangenheitsbewältigung*
when a whole country gets on the couch
to work through their issues with Motherland
and Fatherland. Imagine two different
Monsterwörter to describe that reckoning.

Admit it, you feel *Schadenfreude*
when they get their comeuppance.
What else do you talk about at the *Kaffeeklatsch*
but how the mighty have fallen, tripping
over *Stolpersteine* every day,
as if blind to the past.

There's that reprieve of *Waldeinsamkeit*
when you walk in the woods,
breathing sylvan charm. But then the news
sneaks in the front door behind you.

You could talk about the weather, this *Heisszeit*
of hot, hotter, dead—or how
the *Kummerspeck* of your grief weighs
you down like a trussed hog.

Kristallnacht comes
like a *Geist*
to scare you under the bed
again and never again,
again and again
and again

while the dust mites speak of *Wanderlust,*
but there's no place
else to go.

The Medium Channels Duende

I am no more than a secretary of the invisible thing.
—Czeslaw Milosz

La dueña is the real
mistress of the house,
mischief, a *diãno*
disturbing the peace
under our skin.

She rolls naked
in the snow, white
fire, barking black
sounds like birth.
She infests anthills

and bedroom walls,
a succubus, keening.
As imp and pixie,
she sports horns
and wings, or wings

and barbs, smells
like blood and loam
and luck, both good
and wild. We glimpse
ourselves in her.

She's a *djin* named
Qarinah, a siren
singing the blues.
She is Eutychia,
borne of Nyx, *qi*

and *brio* and *joie*
de vivre. She's Lilith,
a lamia sucking

blood, queen of night.
She lurks, steals

babies by charm
or spell, howls
at the crowning
of the moon.
She is *duende*, the mad

poet in the attic,
who sleepwalks
through trapdoors,
scribbling prophecies.
She is flamenco

incarnate, a *bailaora*
swishing her skirts,
drumming her heels.
She climbs in
through the bottoms

of our feet,
wells our eyes,
her castanets pulsing
live, ululating
off the empty page.

A dead horse

I've kicked my share
of them plenty hard,
training to gallop
into the wind.
As for dead,
I've beaten more
than one more
than once, I admit,
how that whip
becomes bludgeon,
swings from heart
to my mouth until
it squeals every snub
and breach of trust.
I beat and beat them,
before I hang them
out alone to dry,
while the only beast
awakened and rearing
is me.

World Central Kitchen

Passover 2024

The ants
are marching
single
file, their annual
exodus across
faux-granite
counters, up
and down door
jambs, through
the sea of scraps
in my stainless
steel sink. I've
been told to kill
them, a stew
of sugar and boric
acid. A sweet,
merciful death.
But I can't.
Not this year.
Especially not
this year. May all
who are hungry
come. Eat.

My actions are the ground on which I stand;
I am my deeds

Why I Pray in a Faithless World

Because there are more trees
on earth than stars in the Milky Way

Because molecules in ten drops
of water outnumber all those trees

Because we're not born callous—
a baby's most piercing wails in the maternity ward
echo another newborn's distress,
an antiphonal call and response

Because of half an eggshell,
baby blue and chipped, its other half
ingested by the robin's mother—
nature's precise economy

Because words, like pappus,
waft rootless until they find purchase—
tenacious, golden—linking me to you

Because the white-tailed eagle
recolonized the Chernobyl Exclusion Zone,
and the gray whale, once extinct
in the Atlantic, breaches again

And because I, too, have clawed
through core and crust toward starlight

The First Two Questions Are One

The voice in the garden is still reverberating.
—Adin Steinsaltz

In the beginning, there was the third degree—
Where are you?
I assumed He wanted to know
my precise coordinates, my naked
body in space—longitude, latitude.
I could answer, *Approaching Exit 4*
on the Interstate! or *Out back*
in the garden! but I had no compass—
only traces of ambition
(to impart my name as blessing,
to depart my home as novelty)
and a shadow of compassion
for living things after their kind.
I was a terebinth of unknowing
then, without bearings,
a golem fishing for spine.

The second question keeps me up
tossing through news cycles
of exiles and migrations, thirsty
famines, battles of territorial will.
Eve's firstborn posed it at the outset,
ferocious in self-defense:
Am I my brother's keeper?
Am I? That kid bore—still bears—
the hard edges and scaly skins
I've outgrown, as I slither home
toward Eden, a place that's both mother
and the hereafter, and where *Where?*
reeks of authority, insinuating
my backbone, poor in pith and marrow.

Birding With My Sister

She tracks the migration of hummingbirds,
calls to say they were in Philly two days ago,
could arrive today at her lake house in upstate
New York. Her feeders, readied, shine

red with nectar. Last summer she fell
for a blue heron. She'd moor in the middle
of the lake, play a game of dare with him,
refused to part first. She swore he waited

on the banks for her to kayak past
for their rendezvous, and sent me daily
photos of his one-legged posturing.
We joked about this boyfriend, the time

she spent in pursuit. I even googled him,
wondered if *Heron* might break her heart.
But he's a symbol of calm, his visitations
a call for deep breath, pause. Just one

is never a siege. Today I bird with her,
anticipate the dare of charm, tune, shimmer
of flock, the pungent bouquet of truth in wings
chattering with brio and hum. Had I not

been a fish in my other life, I'd adopt her
reverence for flight, for yogic postures
lakefront, for plotting patterns of exodus
and stations of oasis on the migrant

journey. But I am propelled to undulate,
flapping and feeding in the great,
briny school of the deep, not rooted
to land, nor destined for flight.

A seven-year study

predicts that one third
of the world's lakes will lose
their blue as temperatures rise.

Algae will run riot, murking
water to shadow and cloud.
I only mention it because,

at the same time, artists
have a new blue on their palette,
the first in two hundred

years, a pigment more vivid,
more luminous than Crayola's Cerulean sky,
the lapis lazuli of God's footstool,

the glazed cobalt of Ishtar's gate, or even
Wild Blue Yonder. Crayola
christened this latest find, Bluetiful.

Unlike blues that fade with time
like Midnight or Denim,
YInMn—

Yttrium-Indium-Manganese Oxide—
reflects heat and lasts forever,
even when mixed with water.

If You're Lucky

You love that Jane Goodall
writes about hope, despite
all the bad news on your doorstep

like a million species as sitting
ducks on their way to extinction.
You get nature's lust to re-create

itself—how the peregrine falcons
re-nested after the black
air in Sudbury, how the nuked

oleanders in Hiroshima revived,
how the octopus grows
a new arm, the skink a new tail.

But your mind does loop de loops
around Jane's faith in the human
will to resurrect ourselves.

If you're lucky, most of life
is boring. You get up every morning
to pee, turn on the tea kettle,

Zoom through your day.
Sometimes that humdrum
is punctured by breaking news:

an unprecedented storm
bolting up the coast, another
insult from clogged chambers

of Congress, a novel variant
of despotism, or a text
from a friend about her diagnosis.

You recount these aberrations
on your weekly phone calls
with distant relatives, rehash

false memories of good ol' days
on the levee, where Archie
was just some fiction in Queens,

not the guy behind the deli
counter at Safeway who gives
your BLM t-shirt stink eye.

You'd rather shine light—
like Jane—in the nooks
of possibility, slow

dance with faith
in the One above,
face down fear that this

will be the day the music
dies, confident in the radiating
powers of your friend's treatment—

happy for a while, joking
full throttle with the guy
behind the deli counter.

This Small, Wide World

I hear the side door of her truck slide open across the street
& think *mail.* I flash on Meg Ryan & that restaurant scene,
& my own last climactic delivery. Wrong film, I know,

but with the click of our mailbox lid, I think of all the hand-
written notes & holiday missives no one writes anymore,
the sympathy cards Hallmark doesn't make for job loss

or climate grief, those thin blue envelopes from pen pals
in Kenya & Israel I lost touch with & can't find on Facebook,
but whose stamps I steamed off & saved. Through the window

I watch Bertie head up the hill, lean & tan, her telltale
button-up the same blue as those bygone aerogrammes—
& unwrinkled—a bundle of mail in her arms. I imagine hail

& sleet, global warming, the pandemic, how she shows up
even though it was never the USPS motto, how Herodotus
wrote that about the Persians in 500 BCE, including the word

gloom on his list of what could never deter such speedy couriers.
When she's out of sight, I open the front door, slip my hand
into the mailbox adorned with a #SaveThePostOffice sticker I got

from MoveOn to show her love thirty-three American crises ago.
Among the junk, a glossy 6x9. I've just retired, but for a blink
of my eye, I consider applying, usps.com/careers. *Sense*

of service to the community. Diverse workplace. When I
was twelve, I asked about a summer job at the local post office.
The clerk said I was too young for civil service, & besides,

I should set my sights higher. Higher? I thought. I show
my husband the ad, tell him how I need to be of service. Oh, yeah?
he says, leading me upstairs. I hear Bertie start up her truck

to drive away. Someone down the block may receive a colorful
stamp from a faraway land. I conjure the ride-through
at the World's Fair when I was four. *It's a small world* is wide

and glorious and I want it—a safari in Kenya, a close-up
of a blue-footed boobie in the Galápagos, a pilgrimage
on the El Camino, a tête-à-tête with the Dalai Lama

in Dharamshala. But my husband wants to keep it local,
like our vegetables, wishes for a world so small & intimate,
that all I'd want to do is deliver his mail.

The Little Prince Said It First

What is essential is invisible to the eye—
knowing this to be true, troubled
by what I saw straight-on
and sideways in my periphery,
I set my eyes on building heaven
on earth, as naive, some thought,

as that golden-curled space
traveler with his signature scarf.
By then I had words for *calling*
and *sacred,* for *glory* and *grace,*
and for the animal spirit galloping
in me, its invitation to wrangle

clouds into patterns of meaning,
ride dolphins bareback into town,
defender of children and other living
things, and to lie belly-up
like a cat, exposed, because students
want to see how the rabbi ties her shoes.

I trained to spelunk in caves
of the heart, certain of the patience
of bulbs below ground. I sniffed hard-
to-reach blessings in crevices
of human grief, even when miles
and months away, like a polar bear

on the scent of a seal three feet
under ice. By then I knew synesthesia
was a paradox of spiritual
wholeness, like John Locke's
blind man who smelled the color
scarlet when he heard a trumpet blast.

I, too, touch and taste red when the alarm
rouses me to the world ablaze,
the Garden distant. That's when I miss
my mother and think of the rose
alone in the bell jar, the one
we're all called to raise.

1HLY 48

There was the musty bungalow in Beach Haven
where we bunked each summer for a week,
my father fishing his way from worries
left bobbing on his store shelves.

My mother still stood over a stove except for our Sunday
brunch at a sagging Victorian. Around a table for five
on its spacious porch, we fed on M&M pancakes,
red and orange leaching our tongues, our lips.

Later, I paddled out to wait on a breaker, then rode
to shore or tumbled in the undertow. I emerged
coughing and triumphant, lips blue with cold,
wondering if anyone would notice if I drowned.

To dissemble our sadness, we played the license plate
game on the Garden State driving home, tuned
to our mother's swelling despair, the sameness
that awaited us. We called out *Captain!* or *Carpet!*

when we spotted CPT, strutted multisyllabics
like *Magnificent!* if it were MGI. Today, on a July beach
kind of day—though I live below the mountain where,
on a snowy day, Melville dreamed a white whale—

the Prius in front of me calls those car rides to mind, and *Holy,*
holy, holy!—not *hourly,* nor *hillbilly,* nor *honestly*—drips
from my lips as prayer, sure even those numerals hold mystery
I can't yet break, the whole world full of glory.

The Rabbi and I

endorse checks with identical signatures,

leave the same fingerprint wherever we touch.
But she's the one to glean glints of silver and prismed

arcs of color in sewer drains, while I regard shadows
gathered like rumors under every streetlamp, broken

or not, and peek over our shoulder at corners
you'd find in slasher flicks. The Rabbi projects authority

on the walls where I'm a mere bluebonnet, budding
under my own brim to avoid her sun.

The Rabbi keeps her shit together as clients
(on a quest for miracle or revelation) leak

their classified secrets of shame and sorrow,
sometimes in a single bound, sometimes doled out

like accounts payable, one small disbursement
at a time. The couples—stung and nettled—spill

chapters and verses of their sex lives into the upholstery
while I perform mental somersaults on her shoulder,

wonder what she'll draw next
from her rolling index of proverbs and cautions.

I brandish pom-poms at her every touché
and will her, at times, to spew expletives as I do.

My sororal doppelgänger delivers whole sentences
on a silver-tongued platter to hungry crowds

of spectators—inhabits Audre Lorde's erotic
as power electrified, while I, her unassuming

Clark Kent, am hamstrung by the wisdom
she strives to confer, too afraid of mansplaining to speak

aloud in public. She never joins me in the pool
with her *thou-shalt-nots,* though she'd love to see mine

drown there, resuscitated as *halleluyahs*.
And while her husband claims to be her most faithful

congregant, I rarely let her in our bedroom.
She jokes that she's a better "professional"

than a "personal." Had our brother called her at the office,
rather than me at home before he jumped

from that bridge, he might still be two-stepping
in his cowboy boots at some bar with his husband.

So if—when—you need counsel, best try the Rabbi
at work during business hours. She's there, waiting.

The Great Big Indelible Tent of Us

An indigo blue cat sprawled from one woman's
left shoulder to her elbow vertically, its head
facing down, about to enter the next of its nine lives.
I wondered if I'd wandered into the wrong concert,

surrounded by tattooed women at Tanglewood, not
the classical music groupies I expected on a Sunday
morning. I approached her blanket for a close-up,
her tattoo resembling a giraffe standing tall, from afar.

I told her it was beautiful anyway. Behind her,
a black mandala—geometrically intricate, something
to get lost inside of like a maze—graced a thigh, visible
below the hem of a young short-haired woman's

skort. I pondered my aversion to tattoos, how inked
skin hints of Auschwitz, plus the biblical taboo—
why that specific *thou shalt not* today enraged me,
all the constraints on my body, its autonomy—

how I should reconsider and get one of my own
in defiance, a plague on the house of conformity.
And then Coney Island blocked my view of the string
quartet onstage. Knee to ankle, she transported me

to Brooklyn, her legs brimming all the way round with Ferris
wheels and roller coasters, a big red-and-white tent,
cotton candy, each limb a merry-go-round at rest. I wanted
to get up from my folding chair to lie on the ground

between her legs for the intimate details, but she moved
to the shady side of the lawn and I lost contact
with the hot air balloon of her, which rose inside of me
until I could look down on myself from above.

Chewing the Five Zen Remembrances

You're neither Buddhist nor Hindu, but here you are,
kneeling on a zafu, slack-jawed, fighting sleep.

You watch the breath at the center of your universe—nostrils,
diaphragm, belly, expand/deflate like a real yogi, growling.

When the woman next to you squirms, wheezing, old monkey
mind drops upside down from the ceiling, grilling your motives.

You're there for nirvana, to disgorge the huddled sentries
from their watchtowers in your mind, perhaps a few enlightened

nights of sleep. You want to stand in tree pose without teetering
and to sit cross-legged without cramps. You ruminate

on those Zen fates one by one, a gastronomic ploy to get you
back to basics like unleavened bread: how you're of the nature

to grow old or ill, to ingest small deaths—losing, always losing—
before the final one, your own. You know you can't hold on

to anything for dear life, except for these common-sensicals
that rouse you from your torpor, roaring to be welcomed. Mother

gone, father gone, brother, too, gone. You plant your feet, stack
your hips, knees, ankles. You drop your shoulders, tailbone.

You'll play mountain, unfazed by wind or time. You breathe in
for five counts, *I, too, am of the nature to die,* then empty out,

I must be parted from all I love. On your knees, you extend
your arms, a child's pose over their graves. You practice tree,

growing roots so you no longer fall. But monkey rattles
your branches each time you nibble at the fifth

of the Upajjhatthana Sutta. It sticks in your craw, breath trapped,
like when your morning prayer—*My soul is pure*—would make

you gag. Monkey see. Monkey laugh. Monkey-you skeptical
that the crumbs of your deeds—what's left of you at the final

tally—can turn your monkey self to *mensch*. Your lungs fill, empty,
doing their business, and you keep chewing to get yourself right.

Notes

The *Upajjhatthana Sutta* ("Subjects for Contemplation") is a Buddhist discourse that contains the Five Remembrances. The Buddha said that "these are the five facts that one should reflect on often" in the belief that they would lead to freedom and awakening.

The quotation in "Prokofiev's First Violin Sonata" (page 27) is the composer's remark about the scales in the first and fourth movements.

About the Author

Pamela Wax is an ordained rabbi who has worked as a congregational rabbi, a pastoral counselor, and an adult educator whose articles and essays on topics of feminism and Jewish spirituality have been published in numerous books and periodicals. She is author of two previous poetry collections, *Walking the Labyrinth* (Main Street Rag, 2022) and *Starter Mothers* (Finishing Line Press, 2023). Her poems, published in over 60 literary journals, have received three Best of the Net nominations, and awards from *Crosswinds, Paterson Literary Review, Poets' Billow, Oberon,* the Ruben Rose Memorial Poetry Competition, and the Robinson Jeffers Tor House. Pam lives in the Northern Berkshires of Massachusetts.

S
Sheila-Na-Gig Editions

www.ingramcontent.com/pod-product-compliance
Ingram Content Group UK Ltd.
Pitfield, Milton Keynes, MK11 3LW, UK
UKHW041846200726
13854UKWH00005BA/2284